A LITTLE BOOK OF LEDWIDGE

A Little Book of Ledwidge

A Selection of the Poems and Letters of
FRANCIS LEDWIDGE

Compiled by
JOHN QUINN

With an Assessment by
SEAMUS HEANEY

VERITAS

Published 2017 by
Veritas Publications
7–8 Lower Abbey Street
Dublin 1
Ireland
publications@veritas.ie
www.veritas.ie

ISBN 978 1 84730 783 5

10 9 8 7 6 5 4 3 2 1

'In Memoriam Francis Ledwidge' by Seamus Heaney is from *Field Work*,
published by Faber & Faber Ltd, 1979. Copyright © Seamus Heaney.

A catalogue record for this book is available from the British Library.

Designed by Padraig McCormack, Veritas Publications
Printed in Ireland by Anglo Printers Ltd, Drogheda

To mark the centenary of the poet's death
on 31 July 1917 during the third Battle of Ypres

'And I was wondering in my mind
How many would remember me ...'

Francis Ledwidge, 'On Dream Water'

❧ Contents

❧ Preface

Although he is my fellow countyman and although I am old enough to remember coming across some of his poems in my primary school texts, Francis Ledwidge did not really swim into my ken until thirty years ago when the centenary of his birth was celebrated in his native Slane in 1987. My newfound interest resulted in two radio documentaries for RTÉ – one on his life and work, 'The Helpless Child of Circumstance' and one on the centenary celebrations, 'In Pleasant Meads'. When I began writing for children, Ledwidge became a character in my first book, *The Summer of Lily and Esme*, and the book was dedicated to him:

> And I was wondering in my mind
> How many would remember me.

How many remember Francis Ledwidge on the centenary of his death? And how many of more recent generations have ever heard of him? To remind the former and to introduce the latter to the talents of 'the poet of the blackbird', I have assembled this little celebratory volume – a selection of his poems and excerpts from his letters from the battlefront. There is also the added bonus of an assessment of Ledwidge by Seamus Heaney and Heaney's own wonderful poem in tribute to Ledwidge.

I hope this collection will bring a new awareness of the 'poet of the blackbird' on this the centenary of his tragic death.

> Tomorrow will be loud with war,
> How will I be accounted for?

John Quinn, January 2017

❧ Introduction

Francis Joseph Ledwidge was born in a labourer's cottage at Janeville, Slane, Co. Meath on 19 August, 1887. He was the eighth of nine children born to Patrick and Ann Ledwidge. Patrick died when Francis was four and Anne laboured in the fields to provide for her growing family. On leaving primary school, 'Frank' worked on the roads, on farms, as a shop boy, an office worker and in a copper mine. He had dabbled in poetry from his school days but, under the patronage of Lord Dunsany, his poetic career flourished and three anthologies were eventually published: *Songs of the Fields*, *Songs of Peace* and *Last Songs*.

Frank Ledwidge joined the Irish Volunteers in 1913 but, to the surprise of many, he enlisted in the Royal Inniskilling Fusiliers a year later to take part in the Great War. He saw action in the disaster that was Gallipoli, in Serbia and ultimately in France. He was killed in action on the first day of the Battle of Passchendaele on 31 July 1917. He was twenty-nine years of age. Although he had witnessed the horrors of war, his poetry never reflected them. He preferred to write about the things of home and he is known as the 'Poet of the Blackbird' and 'the Poet of the Boyne'.

❧ Home and Schooling

'I bless the God who such a mother gave
This poor bird-hearted singer of a day'

I am of a family who were ever soldiers and poets … I have heard my mother say many times that the Ledwidges were once a great people in the land and she has shown with a sweep of her hand green hills and wide valleys where sheep are folded, which still bear the marks of dead industry, and once this was all ours.[1]

To my mother, the first singer I knew[2]

My Mother

God made my mother on an April day,
From sorrow, and the mist along the sea,
Lost birds' and wanderers' songs and ocean spray,
And the moon loved her wandering jealously.

Beside the ocean's din she combed her hair,
Singing the nocturne of the passing ships,
Before her earthly lover found her there
And kissed away the music from her lips.

---

1 All prose passages, unless otherwise indicated, are from Ledwidge's letter to the American academic, Professor Lewis Chase

2 Ledwidge's dedication of his first book

She came unto the hills and saw the change
That brings the swallow and the geese in turns.
But there was not a grief she deemed strange,
For there is that in her which always mourns.

Kind heart she has for all on hill or wave
Whose hopes grew wings like ants to fly away.
I bless the God who such a mother gave
This poor bird-hearted singer of a day.

❧

*She taught me to listen to and appreciate the blackbird's song
and when I grew to love it beyond all others, she said it was
because I was born in a blackbird's nest and had its blood in
my veins ...*

❧

*These stories told at my mother's doorstep, in the owl's light,
were the first things I remember, except perhaps the old songs
which she sang to me, so full of romance, love and sacrifice.*

❧

❧ Desire in Spring

I love the cradle songs that mothers sing
In lonely places when the twilight drops,
The slow endearing melodies that bring
Sleep to the weeping lids, and, when she stops,
I love the roadside birds upon the tops
Of dusty hedges in a world of Spring.

And when the sunny rain drips from the edge
Of midday wind, and meadows lean one way,
And a long whisper passes thro' the sedge,
Beside the broken water let me stay,
While these old airs upon my memory play,
And silent changes colour up the hedge.

∽

I was one day punished in school for crying and that punishment ever after haunted the master like an evil dream, for I was only crying over Goldsmith's 'Deserted Village', which an advanced class had been reading aloud.

∽

There was a literary society for juveniles run thro' the pages of a Dublin weekly and I soon became a member of this. In all the competitions for which I entered I carried off the prize and soon had a decent library of the books which interest children. Odd halfpennies which I got for some message run for the neighbours accumulated in time and were exchanged for The Arabian Nights, Robinson Crusoe, Don Quixote, *and the poems of Keats and Longfellow. My admiration for Longfellow began early and I could recite passages from* The Golden Legend *at eight years. I loved the series of metaphors in* Hiawatha *beginning:*

> *'Fiercely the red sun descending.*
> *Burned his way along the mountains.'*

but thought nothing in all the world as wonderful as Shakespeare's fairy song:

> *'Full fathoms five thy father lies.*
> *Of his bones are coral made.'*

While I was still at school many silly verses left my pen, written either for my own amusement, or the amusement of my companions. Indeed I left many an exercise unfinished, hurrying over some thought that shaped itself into rhyme.

❧ Stanley Hill

In Stanley Hill the bees are loud
And loud a river wild,
And there, as wayward as a cloud,
I was a little child.

I knew not how mistrustful heart
Could lure with hidden wile,
And wound it in a fateful part
With dark and sudden guile.

And yet for all I've known and seen
Of Youth and Truth reviled,
On Stanley Hill the grass is green
And I am still a child.

I have always been very quiet and bashful and a great mystery in my own place. I avoided the evening play of neighbouring children to find some secret place in a wood by the Boyne and there imagine fairy dances and hunts, fires and feasts. I saw curious shapes in shadows and clouds and loved to watch the change of the leaves and the flowers. I heard voices in the rain and the wind and strange whisperings in the waters. I loved all wandering people and things

and several times tried to become part of a gypsy caravan. I read of Troy and Nineveh and the nomads of the east and the mystery of the Sahara. I wrote wander songs for cuckoos and winter songs for the robin. I hated gardens where gaudy flowers were trained in rows but loved the wild things of change and circumstance. One by one my other brothers and sisters left school for the world until there were left only myself and my youngest brother and mother.

'On certain occasions Frank would be a bit indiscreet and correct old Master Madden, on a matter of grammar, maybe. The old man didn't like this at all and he was ever after on edge with Frank. However, when Frank's poems began to appear in the local paper – the *Drogheda Independent* – later on, old Madden would go into the pub at the weekend, take out the paper, read out Frank's poem and say 'I taught that boy!'

Joe Ledwidge

Meanwhile the years were coming over me and I began to realise that man cannot live by dreams. I had no more to learn in national school at fourteen, so I strapped up my books and laid them away with the cobwebs and the dust.

I read and studied the poets of England from the age of Chaucer to Swinburne. I thirsted for travel and adventure and longed to see the Italy of Shelley and the Greece of Byron. But the poetry of Keats and his sad life appealed to me most ...

෨

❦ Work

'Above me smokes the little town
With its whitewashed walls and roofs of brown'

'He worked for local farmers after leaving school. There were no other jobs going. Then for a time he worked as a foreman on the roads with Meath County Council. There was a copper mine in Beauparc at the time and he worked there for a while, but it didn't last long. He tried to organise a workers' union but when he did the mine-owners fired him ...'

Joe Ledwidge

❧ To a Linnet in a Cage

When Spring is in the fields that stained your wing,
And the blue distance is alive with song,
And finny quiets of the gabbling spring
Rock lilies red and long,
At dewy daybreak, I will set you free
In ferny turnings of the woodbine lane,
Where faint-voiced echoes leave and cross in glee
The hilly swollen plain.

In draughty houses you forget your tune,
The modulator of the changing hours.

You want the wide air of the moody noon
And the slanting evening showers.
So I will loose you, and your song shall fall
When morn is white upon the dewy pane,
Across my eyelids, and my soul recall
From worlds of sleeping pain.

*My mother apprenticed me to a Dublin grocer and sent me off
one spring morning with many tears and blessings and nothing
of anything else. I could not bear brick horizons and my dreams
were calling me home. I wrote 'Behind the Closed Eye' and
scarcely was the last line written when I stole out the back door
and set my face for home. I arrived home at six a.m., dusty and
hungry after a thirty mile walk.[3]*

☙ Behind the Closed Eye

I walk the old frequented ways
That wind around the tangled braes,
I live again the sunny days
Ere I the city knew.

---

3   Letter by Ledwidge to Professor Chase

And scenes of old again are born,
The woodbine lassoing the thorn,
And drooping Ruth-like in the corn
The poppies weep the dew.

Above me in their hundred schools
The magpies bend their young to rules,
And like an apron full of jewels
The dewy cobweb swings.

And frisking in the stream below
The troutlets make the circles flow,
And the hungry crane doth watch them grow
As a smoker does his rings.

Above me smokes the little town,
With its whitewashed walls and roofs of brown
And its octagon spire toned smoothly down
As the holy minds within.

And wondrous impudently sweet,
Half of him passion, half conceit,
The blackbird calls adown the street
Like the piper of Hamelin.

I hear him, and I feel the lure
Drawing me back to the homely moor,
I'll go and close the mountain's door
On the city's strife and din.

🌿 Lord Dunsany

Edward John Plunkett was the eighteenth Baron of Dunsany and lived in Dunsany Castle, Co. Meath. He was a captain in the Royal Inniskilling Fusiliers during the Great War. He wrote plays, short stories, novels and poetry under the name Lord Dunsany.

'For you love to bring
The true note in and say the wise thing terse'

'He would never have been heard of but for Dunsany. He would never have got to the outside world. There was a local sculptor, a man named Cassidy, who had done very well and he advised Frank to get a position like he had got. Ledwidge followed his advice and wrote to Dunsany.'

Alice Curtayne, Ledwidge's biographer

'I got a letter from a young Irishman enclosing a copy-book full of verses and asking if they were any good. He was Francis Ledwidge. I was astonished by the brilliance of that eye that had looked at the fields of Meath and seen there all the simple birds and flowers, with a vividness that made those pages like a magnifying glass, through which one looked at familiar things seen thus for the first time. I wrote to him greeting him as a true poet, which indeed he was, and his gratitude for that was intense, though quite undeserved; for, as I have said elsewhere, the lark owes nothing to us for knowing that he is a lark. From that time he poured out poems, and was still doing so, and I made a selection from them for his book. These poems were so unexpected and were sent or brought to me so frequently, that they gave me the queer impression that this Irish villager had found some coffer, stored in a golden age, brimful of lyrics and lost long ago.'

Lord Dunsany

'Dunsany gave him great encouragement. He invited Frank up to Dunsany Castle. Frank was very pleased with the interview he had with Dunsany, who treated him very well. He became a kind of brother to him. Frank had access to Dunsany's library. He had certain instructions from Dunsany which he found easy to follow – to cut out things such as repetition, and certain expressions. Dunsany told him he must follow his own inspiration and not imitate anybody.'

Joe Ledwidge

☙ The Homecoming of the Sheep

The sheep are coming home to Greece,
Hark the bells on every hill!
Flock by flock, and fleece by fleece,
Wandering wide a little piece
Thro' the evening red and still,
Stopping where the pathways cease,
Cropping with a hurried will.

Thro' the cotton bushes low
Merry boys with shouldered crooks
Close them in a single row,
Shout among them as they go
With one bell-ring o'er the brooks.
Such delight you never know
Reading it from gilded books.

Before the early stars are bright
Cormorants and sea-gulls call,
And the moon comes large and white
Filling with a lovely light
The ferny curtained waterfall.
Then sleep wraps every bell up tight
And the climbing moon grows small.

Thanks very much for your two letters received a couple of days ago. Yes, I received your cigarettes all right. We had a busy day with the Turks when they came, but that didn't prevent us from smoking them.

So Songs of the Fields *are out at last. I suppose the critics are blowing warm and cold over them with the same mouth, like the charcoal burner in Aesop's fable. Jenkins sent me a copy. It is a lovely book and quite a decent size, but my best is not in it. That has to come yet. I feel something great struggling in my soul but it can't come until I return; if I don't return it will never come.*

I wish the damn war would end; we are all so sick for the old countries. Still, our hearts are great and we are always ready for anything which may be required of us.

I am writing a poem which I will send you when finished; meanwhile I hope my book sells by thousands. I won't try to thank you for all you have done for me and are doing. You know how grateful I am.[4]

Your letter of 20 February did me more good than all the dirty medicine I have been drinking for the past three months. So you

---

4   Letter to Dunsany from Serbia, where Ledwidge received a copy of his first book in 1915

liked the poem about the sheep? So do I, very much. Did you get the Arab poems? I like these also and the ones I now send, particularly 'The Cobbler'.

I didn't get your books yet. I am eagerly watching for them. I like Matthew Arnold's The Forsaken Merman *and* The Scholar Gypsy. *But I love Keats. I think poor Keats reaches the top of beauty in 'Ode to a Grecian Urn', 'To a Nightingale', and 'Autumn', as well as in several of his beautiful apostrophes in the poem 'Endymion'. I like Keats best of all. I remember years ago praying to Keats for aid.[5]*

✒ The Cobbler of Sari Gueul

A cobbler lives in Sari Gueul
Who has a wise mind, people say.
He sits in his door on a three-legged stool,
Hammering leather all the day.
He laughs with the boys who make such noise
And loves to watch how the children play.
Gladly I'd shuffle my lot in a pool
With that of the cobbler in Sari Gueul.

---

5   Letter to Dunsany from hospital in Cairo, March 1916

Sorrow to him is a ball of wax
That melts in the sun of a cheerful smile
And all his needs are, a box of tacks,
Thread and leather, old boots in a pile.
I would give my art for half of his heart.
Who wants the world with all its guile?
And which of us two is the greatest fool,
Me, or the cobbler of Sari Gueul?[6]

❧

I am too short of paper to send you copies of some poems I have written, but I will be careful of them until an issue takes place if one ever does in this awful place. I wish I could get back for a rest and go to France in the spring. I will never hold out all the winter here as I suffer terribly from rheumatism. The nights when not raining are freezing and one wonders which is the worse for the pains.

Of course you understand that we are quite different from what we have been in your day. We are all weak and sick, but we suffered much.

Would there be any chance of getting home for a month? The doctor will only give one a day's rest, that is no cure for rheumatism when the same day miles of a march have to be done and that night a 'listening post' in some outlandish hollow.

---

6   Written during Ledwidge's retreat from Serbia 1916

When I get paper I will send you copies of my latest work, meanwhile if you could get a holiday for me I would be so grateful, and so would my mother.[7]

'Let us not call him the Burns of Ireland, you who may like this book, nor even the Irish John Clare, though he is more like him, for poets are all incomparable (it is only the versifiers that resemble the great ones), but let us know him by his own individual song: he is the poet of the blackbird.'

From Dunsany's introduction to *Songs of the Fields*

ᥰ A Twilight in Middle March

Within the oak a throb of pigeon wings
Fell silent, and grey twilight hushed the fold,
And spiders' hammocks swung on half-oped things
That shook like foreigners upon our cold.
A gypsy lit a fire and made a sound
Of moving tins, and from an oblong moon

---

7   Letter to Dunsany from Serbia, 1915

The river seemed to gush across the ground
To the cracked metre of a marching tune.

And then three syllables of melody
Dropped from a blackbird's flute, and died apart
Far in the dewy dark. No more but three,
Yet sweeter music never touched a heart
'Neath the blue domes of London. Flute and reed,
Suggesting feelings of the solitude
When will was all the Delphi I would heed,
Lost like a wind within a summer wood
From little knowledge where great sorrows brood.

'Dunsany's patronage was very important to Ledwidge. The transition from the unseen life of Slane to the more visible milieu of Dublin, where he was introduced to McDonagh, AE (George Russell), and maybe even Pearse, meant that his self-estimation must have risen considerably, his confidence boosted and his reputation helped. Dunsany's contribution was a generous and selfless act.'

Seamus Heaney

❧ Love [1]

Ellie Vaughey from the Hill of Slane was Frank Ledwidge's first love. However, she spurned him and married another, dying in childbirth within the year.

'I look across the edge of things that were
And you are lovely in the April ways'

From 'Thoughts at the Trysting-Stile'

I wait the calling of the orchard maid
Inly I feel that she will come in blue,
With yellow on her hair, and two curls strayed
Out of her comb's loose stocks, and I shall steal
Behind and lay my hands upon her eyes,
'Look not, but be my Psyche!'
                                        And her peal
Of laughter will ring far, and as she tries
For freedom I will call her names of flowers
That climb up walls; then thro' the twilight hours
We'll talk about the loves of ancient queens,
And kisses like wasp-honey, false and sweet,
And how we are entangled in love's snares
Like wind-looped flowers.

A Song

My heart has flown on wings to you, away
In the lonely places where your footsteps lie
Full up of stars when the short showers of day
Have passed like ancient sorrows. I would fly
To your green solitude of woods to hear

You singing in the sounds of leaves and birds;
But I am sad below the depth of words
That nevermore we two shall draw anear.

Had I but wealth of land and bleating flocks
And barnfuls of the yellow harvest yield,
And a large house with climbing hollyhocks
And servant maidens singing in the field,
You'd love me, but I own no roaming herds,
My only wealth is songs of love for you,
And now that you are lost I may pursue
A sad life deep below the depth of words.

꙳

꙳ The Broken Tryst

The dropping words of larks, the sweetest tongue
That sings between the dusks, tell all of you;
The bursting white of Peace is all along
Wing-ways, and pearly droppings of the dew
Emberyl the cobwebs' greyness, and the blue
Of hiding violets, watching for your face,
Listen for you in every dusky place.
You will not answer when I call your name,
But in the fog of blossom do you hide

To change my doubts into a red-faced shame
By'n by when you are laughing by my side?
Or will you never come, or have you died,
And I in anguish have forgotten all?
And shall the world now end and the heavens fall?

❧ The Death of Love

We stood and watched the full-blown moon arise,
And then I felt her pulse strong in her palm:
I knew the storm was over, and the calm
Would empty out the sorrow in her eyes.
And I then said 'Since this is Love's demise
Our hearts have tears her beauty to embalm
We'll leave her by forever with a psalm
Of her lost promise, in our memories
And there she shall be clothed in the white
Of our best moments, and the heart shall wear
A path around her grave.' A little sail
Stood on the middle of the moon's huge light
And for a little while went trembling there
Believing how the world was waxing pale.

From 'After My Last Song'

I'm wild for wandering to the far-off places
Since one forsook me whom I held most dear.
I want to see new wonders and new faces
Beyond East seas; but I will win back here
When my last song is sung, and veins are cold
As thawing snow, and I am grey and old.

From 'A Memory'

No, not more silent does the spider stitch
A cobweb on the fern, nor fogdrops fall
On sheaves of harvest when the night is rich
With moonbeams, than the spirits of delight
Walk the dark passages of Memory's hall.
We feel them not, but in the wastes of night
We hear their low-voiced mediums, and we rise
To wrestle old Regrets, to see old faces,
To meet and part in old tryst-trodden places
With breaking heart, and emptying of eyes.

To One Dead

A blackbird singing
On a moss-upholstered stone,
Bluebells swinging,
Shadows wildly blown,
A song in the wood,
A ship on the sea,
The song was for you
And the ship was for me.

A blackbird singing
I hear in my troubled mind,
Bluebells swinging
I see in a distant wind.
But sorrow and silence
Are the wood's threnody,
The silence for you
And the sorrow for me.

❧ Friendship

Ledwidge developed a close friendship with Matty McGoona, who worked as a printer with the *Meath Chronicle*. Matty was a well-read and self-educated man and the two friends were part of a group called 'Grattan's Parliament' which discussed politics and other topics.

'Come often, friend; with welcome and surprise
We'll greet you from the sea or from the town'

❧ To My Best Friend

I love the wet-lipped wind that stirs the hedge
And kisses that bend flowers that drooped for rain,
That stirs the poppy on the sun-burned ledge
And like a swan dies singing, without pain.
The golden bees go buzzing down to stain
The lilies' frills, and the blue harebell rings,
And the sweet blackbird in the rainbow sings.

Deep in the meadow I would sing a song,
The shallow brook my tuning-fork, the birds
My masters, and the boughs they hop along
Shall mark my time: but there shall be no words
For lurking Echo's mock; an angel herds
Words that I may not know, within, for you,
Words for the faithful meet, the good and true.

'The idea of self-improvement was in the air for young fellows at that time. Ledwidge and McGoona walked round the hedges and ditches and found the names for flowers. There was in that whole generation part of the British turn-of-the-century movement for the self-improvement

of the working man. That movement was afoot in
Ireland and Ledwidge was part of that sociological
moment also.'

Seamus Heaney

✑ To Matty McGoona

(Who came one day when we were all gloomy and
cheered us with sad music)

We were all sad and could not weep,
Because our sorrow had not tears:
You came a silent thing like Sleep,
And stole away our fears.

Old memories knocking at each heart
Troubled us with the world's great lie:
You sat a little way apart
And made a fiddle cry.

And April with her many showers
Came laughing up the fields again:
White wings went flashing thro' the hours
So lately full of pain.

And rivers full of little lights
Came down the fields of waving green:
Our immemorial delights
Stole in on us unseen.

For this may Good Luck let you loose
Upon her treasures many years,
And Peace unfurl her flag of truce
To any threat'ning fears.

How are you this one hundred years? I know trouble has lain against you like an incubus and I felt for you many and many a time. I hope you are in good cheer again. I wish you could call a cabinet meeting of Grattan's Parliament and discuss terms of peace with the warring powers. Or has it been abolished and the old members fled? Christ! Matty it's hard thinking on the old times. The pleasant Sundays we used to spend and the hopes we entertained! Their memories follow me like so many Nemeses, and I often feel like a reprobate who has committed his last sin and dare not hope any more for absolution. I am glad we are going to the war, it will cheer me up, it will dispel these thoughts which are at war with me so long. Ellie Vaughey got married! That was a great blow, perhaps the greatest of all. I am going to try for a day home

*Patrick's Day. If I manage it, could you come to Slane? I
want to see you so badly.*

*How is your Pegasus? And how is the violin? Do you ever
play sweet music now? Every time you play 'The Blackbird'
think on me. I love that tune and snatches of it sing in my
memory an odd time like ghosts haunting an old garden. My
memory is no more than an old garden now full of the withered
flowers of a dead summer.*

Your affectionate friend in trouble, Frank.[8]

&

To One Who Comes Now and Then

> When you come in, it seems a brighter fire
> Crackles upon the hearth invitingly,
> The household routine which was wont to tire
> Grows full of novelty.
>
> You sit upon our home-upholstered chair
> And talk of matters wonderful and strange,
> Of books, and travel, customs old which dare
> The gods of Time and Change.

---

8   Letter to Matty McGoona, March 1915. 'Pegasus' was his bicycle

Till we with inner word our care refute
Laughing that this our bosoms yet assails,
While there are maidens dancing to a flute
In Andalusian vales.

And sometimes from my shelf of poems you take
And secret meanings to our hearts disclose,
As when the winds of June the mid bush shake
We see the hidden rose.

And when the shadows muster, and each tree
A moment flutters, full of shutting wings,
You take the fiddle and mysteriously
Wake wonders on the strings.

And in my garden, grey with misty flowers,
Low echoes fainter than a beetle's horn
Fill all the corners with it, like sweet showers
Of bells, in the owl's morn.

Come often, friend, with welcome and surprise
We'll greet you from the sea or from the town;
Come when you like and from whatever skies
Above you smile or frown.[9]

---

9 Written for Matty McGoona in Ypres, nine days before Ledwidge's death

Politics and Going to War (1914-1915)

'When I am back from wand'ring
It's the strange man I'll be'

'He was very nationally-minded indeed. He was a
Sinn Féiner when Sinn Féin was only in its infancy.
Old Madden, the teacher, was a Sinn Féiner and
Frank was probably influenced by him too.'

Joe Ledwidge

*Some of the people who know me least imagine that I joined
the Army because I knew men were struggling for higher ideals
and great emprises, and I could not sit idle to watch them make
for me a more beautiful world. They are mistaken. I joined the
British Army because she stood between Ireland and an enemy
common to our civilisation and I would not have her say that she
defended us while we did nothing at home but pass resolutions. I
am sorry that party politics should ever divide our tents but am
not without hope that a new Ireland will arise from her ashes
in the ruins of Dublin, like the phoenix, with one purpose, one
aim, one ambition.*[10]

10   Letter to Professor Chase

I was waiting a few days to see how I would like a soldier's life before writing to you.

I am having a royal fine time. I only parade one hour per day, the other six I spend in the quartermaster's store as clerk, for which I receive extra pay and mess with clerks in a place specially allotted to them. For breakfast we get tea, bread, butter, fish sometimes, or steak, always something; for dinner beef, vegetables, and afterwards rice. For tea fish again and usually a pineapple. You can see I am not so badly off after all. I see Lord Dunsany every day, and in the evening we meet in his quarters and discuss poetry, the thing that matters.

Dunsany saw to it that I was not sent to Tralee, as an excuse he brought forward the fact of my being an Irish Volunteer and therefore had a certain amount of training. At the recreation rooms on Saturday night next I am giving a reading from some of my embryo books. We will soon be leaving here for the north of Ireland to a shooting range there, and from thence to the seat of war. I look forward to poetry and fame after the war and feel that by joining I am helping to bring about peace and the old sublimity of which the world has been robbed.[11]

⌖

---

11   Letter to Paddy Healy, a friend in Slane

My Dear Bobby,

I have thought of you many and many a time and the splendid mornings we used to go shooting. This life is a great change to me, and one which somehow I cannot become accustomed to. I have lived too much amongst the fields and the rivers to forget that I am anything else other than 'the Poet of the Blackbird'.

However I am not a bad soldier so far. I have scored nineteen out of a possible twenty at the firing range and am in the first drilling platoon and about to move either to France or Egypt in December. We have not a bad time here at all. The only thing we detest is route marching, but even here we are not badly off. We rise at about seven in the morning although reveille goes at six … When not on a route march we do company drill and gymnasium. We have plenty of time to ourselves and are well looked after. I am glad I joined tho' sometimes homesick, but fame and poetry will come again (D.V.).[12]

---

12   Letter to Bobby Anderson, a friend in Slane

⟨⟩ Crocknaharna

On the heights of Crocknaharna
(Oh, the lure of Crocknaharna)

On a morning fair and early
Of a dear remembered May,
There I heard a colleen singing
In the brown rocks and the grey.
She, the pearl of Crocknaharna,
Crocknaharna, Crocknaharna,
Wild with gulls is Crocknaharna
Twenty hundred miles away.

On the heights of Crocknaharna,
(Oh, thy sorrow Crocknaharna)
On an evening dim and misty
Of a cold November day,
There I heard a woman weeping
In the brown rocks and the grey.
Oh, the pearl of Crocknaharna
(Crocknaharna, Crocknaharna),
Black with grief is Crocknaharna
Twenty hundred miles away.[13]

---

13 Written aboard the S.S. Novian, bound for Gallipoli

✐ To My Little Nephew Seumas

I will bring you all the colours
Of the snail's house when I come,
And shells that you may listen
To a distant ocean's hum.
And from the rainbow's bottom
I will bring you coloured lights
To scare away the banshees
That cry in the nights.

And I will sing you strange songs
Of places far away,
Where little moaning waters
Have wandered wild astray.
Till you shall see the bell flowers
Shaking in the breeze,
Thinking they are ringing them
The short way to the seas.

When I come back from wand'ring
It's the strange man I'll be,
And first you'll be a bit afraid
To climb upon my knee.
But when you see the rare gifts
I've gathered you, it seems

You'll lean your head upon me
And travel in your dreams.

✒ In the Mediterranean – Going to the War

Lovely wings of gold and green
Flit about the sounds I hear,
On my window when I lean
To the shadows cool and clear.

Roaming, I am listening still,
Bending, listening overlong,
In my soul a steadier will,
In my heart a newer song.

❧ Nature

'I could find the truth of Beauty
In the fields I left behind'

☙ May

She leans across an orchard gate somewhere,
Bending from out the shadows to the light,
A dappled spray of blossom in her hair
Studded with dew-drops lovely from the night.
She smiles to think how many hearts she'll smite
With beauty ere her robes fade from the lawn.
She hears the robin's cymbals with delight,
The skylarks in the rosebush of the dawn.

For her the cowslip rings its yellow bell,
For her the violets watch with wide blue eyes.
The wandering cuckoo doth its clear name tell
Thro' the white mist of blossoms where she lies
Painting a sunset for the western skies.
You'd know her by her smile and by her tear
And by the way the swift and martin flies,
Where she is south of these wild days and drear.

❧

An Invitation

Come where the hills are heaped together
For the winds are glistening with wings
And Autumn's dull flowers droop and wither
Where, down by the North, the last leaf swings.

I know where a bright well gurgles up
Looping the ferns with a shining tress
And the wild convolvulus reaches her cup
Out on the bee-glad sunniness.

And there we may learn of flower and wing
The true delight of her seasons four,
As the last leaf down on the north wind swings
And the south throws open her warm blue door.

Spring

Once more the lark with song and speed
Cleaves through the dawn, his hurried bars
Fall, like the flute of Ganymede
Twirling and whistling from the stars.

The primrose and the daffodil
Surprise the valleys, and wild thyme
Is sweet on every little hill,
When lambs come down at folding time.

In every wild place now is heard
The magpie's noisy house, and through
The mingled tunes of many a bird
The ruffled wood-dove's gentle coo.

Sweet by the river's noisy brink
The water-lily bursts her crown,
The kingfisher comes down to drink
Like rainbow jewels falling down.

And when the blue and grey entwine
The daisy shuts her golden eye,
And peace wraps all those hills of mine
Safe in my dearest memory.

❧ June

Broom out the floor now, lay the fender by,
And plant this bee-sucked bough of woodbine there,

And let the window down. The butterfly
Floats in upon the sunbeam, and the fair
Tanned face of June, the nomad gypsy, laughs
Above her widespread wares, the while she tells
The farmers' fortunes in the fields, and quaffs
The water from the spider-peopled wells.
The hedges are all drowned in green grass seas,
And bobbing poppies flare like Elmo's light,
While siren-like the pollen-stained bees
Drone in the clover depths. And up the height
The cuckoo's voice is hoarse and broke with joy.
And on the lowland crops the crows make raid,
Nor fear the clappers of the farmer's boy,
Who sleeps, like drunken Noah, in the shade.

And loop this red rose in that hazel ring
That snares your little ear, for June is short
And we must joy in it and dance and sing,
And from here bounty draw her rosy worth.
Ay! Soon the swallows will be flying south,
The wind wheel north to gather in the snow,
Even the roses spilt on youth's red mouth
Will soon blow down the road all roses go.

࿐

✢ Summer at Home

Swath by swath the fallen meadow
Whitens by the river brink,
And the wind comes in a shadow
Where the swallows dip to drink.
Little waves put out their white tongues
Just beyond the mossy weir,
Where the jewelled trout are leaping
And the heron flings his spear.

Water lilies, like the golden
Lamps of old Arabian nights,
Morn sets swinging for the olden
And mysterious river rites,
For Pan still has quiet worship
When the lonely evening dreams
With the white flocks in the valleys
And the dusk about the streams.

Summer now is changing fashion,
Mark the white robes, how she dares.
I, who know her every passion,
Tell her age by what she wears.
There beside her I'd be singing
To her waywardness of mind.

I could find the truth of Beauty
In the fields I left behind.

❧ Loss

'I have had many disappointments in life and many sorrows, but in my saddest moment song came to me and I sang'

❧ The Resurrection

My true love still is all that's fair,
She is flower and blossom blowing free,
For all her silence lying there
She sings a spirit song to me.

New lovers seek her in her bower,
The rain, the dew, the flying wind,
And tempt her out to be a flower,
Which throws a shadow on my mind.

❧

❧ From 'An Old Pain'

'Tis something to have known one day of joy,
Now to remember when the heart is low,
An antidote of thought that will destroy
The asp-bite of Regret. Deep will I drink
By'n by the purple cups that overflow,
And fill the shattered heart's urn to the brink.
But some are dead who laughed! Some scattered are
Around the sultry breadth of foreign zones.
You, with the warm clay wrapt about your bones,
Are nearer to me than the live afar.

My heart has grown as dry as an old crust,
Deep in book lumber and moth-eaten wood,
So long it has forgot the old love lust,
So long forgot the thing that made youth dear,
Two blue love lamps, a heart exceedingly good,
And how, when first I heard that voice ring clear
Among the searing hedges of the plain,
I knew not which from which beyond the corn,
The laughter by the callow twisted thorn,
The jay-thrush whistling in the haws for rain.[14]

⤸ A Little Boy in the Morning

He will not come, and still I wait.
He whistles at another gate
Where angels listen. Ah, I know
He will not come, yet if I go
How shall I know he did not pass
Barefooted in the flowery grass?

---

14 This and 'The Resurrection' (above) are lamenting the loss of Ellie Vaughey

The moon leans on one silver horn
Above the silhouettes of morn,
And from their nest-sills finches whistle
Or stooping pluck the downy thistle.
How is the morn so gay and fair
Without his whistling in its air?

The world is calling, I must go.
How shall I know he did not pass
Barefooted in the shining grass?[15]

ᥱ **Thomas McDonagh**

He shall not hear the bittern cry
In the wild sky, where he is lain,
Nor voices of the sweeter birds
Above the wailing of the rain.

---

15 Lament for the death of a neighbour's child, who would have driven cows past
Ledwidge's house

Nor shall he know when loud March blows
Thro' slanting snows her fanfare shrill
Blowing to flame the golden cup
Of many an upset daffodil.

But when the Dark Cow leaves the moor,
And pastures poor with greedy weeds,
Perhaps he'll hear her low at morn
Lifting her horn in pleasant meads.[16]

🔖 To Mrs Joseph Plunkett

You shall not lack our little praise
If such can win your fair renown.
The halcyon of your lost days
We shall replace with living crown.

We see you not as one of us
Who so lament each little thing,
You profit more by honest loss,
Who lost so much, than song can sing.

---

16   Lament for the executed 1916 Rising leader and a fellow-poet

This you have lost, a heart which bore
An ideal love, an ideal shame,
And earned this thing, for evermore
A noble and splendid name.[17]

---

17   Addressed to the widow of another executed 1916 Rising leader

❧ Gallipoli and Serbia

'No words could describe the cold, the blizzards, the frost and the hunger'

⊷ The Irish in Gallipoli

Where Aegean cliffs with bristling menace front
The Threatening splendour of the isley sea
Lighted by Troy's last shadow, where the first
Hero kept watch and the last Mystery
Shook with dark thunder, hark the battle brunt!
A nation speaks, old Silences are burst.

Neither for lust of glory nor new throne
This thunder and this lightning of our wrath
Waken these frantic echoes, not for these
Our cross with England's mingle, to be blown
On Mammon's threshold; we but war when war
Serves Liberty and Justice, Love and Peace.

Who said that such an emprise could be vain?
Were they not one with Christ Who strove and died?
Let Ireland weep but not for sorrow. Weep
That by her sons a land is sanctified
For Christ Arisen, and angels once again
Come back like exile birds to guard their sleep.

⊷

It is surprising what silly things one thinks of in a big fight. I was lying on one side of a low bush on 19 August, pouring lead into the Turks and for four hours my mind was on the silliest things of home. Once I found myself wondering if a cow that I knew to have a disease called 'timbertongue' had really died. Again, a man on my right who was mortally hit said, 'It can't be far off now' and I began to wonder what it was could not be far off. Then I knew it was death and I kept repeating the dying man's words: 'It can't be far off now'.

But when the Turks began to retreat I realised my position and standing up, I shouted out the range to the men near me and they fell like grass before the scythe, the enemy. It was Hell! Hell! No man thought he would ever return. Just fancy – out of D Company, two-hundred-and-fifty strong, only seventy-six returned. But Heavens, you should know the bravery of these men! Cassidy, standing on a hill with his cap on top of his rifle, shouting at the Turks to come out; stretcher-bearers taking in friend and enemy alike. It was a horrible and a great day. I would not have missed it for worlds.[18]

⁂

It poured rain on us all the long ninety miles we had to march, and what with sleeping in wet clothes, sweating and cooling down,

---

18   Letter to Lord Dunsany re a Gallipoli engagement

I got an attack of Barney Fitzimons back. You have read of our retreat. Shall I ever forget it! We should have left the previous evening but just as we had mustered to go we received word that a French Brigade was almost surrounded higher up and we were called to do a flank attack. We did, and extricated the French, but got into a similar condition ourselves by morning. The Bulgars came on like flies and though we mowed down line after line, they persisted with awful doggedness and finally gave us a bayonet charge which secured their victory. We only just had about two hundred yards to escape by and we had to hold this until next evening and then dribble out as best we could.[19]

❦ Spring and Autumn

Green ripples singing down the corn,
With blossoms dumb the path I tread,
And in the music of the morn
One with wild roses on her head.
Now the green ripples turn to gold
And all the paths are loud with rain,
I with desire am growing old
And full of winter pain.[20]

---

19 Letter to Paddy Healy re a retreat in Serbia
20 Written in Serbia

❦ Love [2]

Ledwidge's second love was Lizzie Healy, sister of his friend Paddy.

'Please, dear Lizzie, send me a flower from the bog, plucked specially for me'

I am sure it is lovely on the bog now. I would very much like to be walking to Carlanstown via Fletcherstown chapel, you with me of course. The people will be planting potatoes down there now and I am certain there is a scent in the air like a feast of wine. From the desk where I am writing this I see through a window across the soldier's recreation ground spire on spire of Dublin, and hear the bells of trams and the shout of all its worry and woe, but my thoughts are in Wilkinstown in the little kitchen where I first took you in my arms.[21]

✑ To Eilish of the Fair Hair

I'd make my heart a harp to play for you
Love songs within the evening dim of day,
Were it not dumb with ache and with mildew
Of sorrow withered like a flower away.
It hears so many calls from homeland places,
So many sighs from all it will remember,
From the pale roads and woodlands where your face is
Like laughing sunlight running thro' December.

---

21   Letter to Lizzie, March 1915

But this it singeth loud above its pain,
To bring the greater ache: whate'er befall
The love that oft-times woke the sweeter strain
Shall turn to you always. And should you call
To pity it some day in those old places
Angels will covet the loud joy that fills it.
But thinking of the by-ways where your face is
Sunlight on other hearts – Ah! how it kills it.

I am back again in the tents of Mars. I can hardly yet realise that I am really back, but it must be true as I see from my office window three or four hundred men at drill. I am back again indeed, or at least my body is, but my soul is on a little road looking across a gate at a girl standing in a doorway. The road is in the village of Wilkinstown and you are the girl at the door.

I am a thousand times the better of my visit to Wilkinstown. I had the happy realisation of hearing you say you would wait for me until I came back and of taking you in my arms. But although I am so much the better for this I am a lot the worse of it, as now, more than ever I know how much I want you and how much I love you. My love for you is as high as the stars.[22]

---

22 Letter to Lizzie, February 1915

☞ Had I a Golden Pound
(after the Irish)

Had I a golden pound to spend,
My love should mend and sew no more.
And I would buy her a little quern,
Easy to turn on the kitchen floor.

And for her windows curtains white,
With birds in flight and flowers in bloom,
To face with pride the road to town,
And mellow down her sunlit room.

And with the silver change we'd prove
The truth of love to life's own end
With hearts the years could but embolden
Had I a golden pound to spend.

*I thought I was out of the army and home again. It was a
beautiful day, flowers everywhere, and birds. I could see all the
old landmarks so loved by me as I crossed the fields down to the
Boyne to meet you. We met at the Mill House. The meeting
was by arrangement. You were sitting on the old paling there
and singing a song I wrote many years ago. When you saw*

*me coming you raced to meet me, and when we had greeted each
other, we walked slowly down by the river, and you were telling
me that you missed me while I was away. You said there was a
void in your life, a sort of feeling making you hope no more for
old aspirations. All our talk was of the past. I wonder why. It
was a beautiful dream and when I wakened I was lonesome. I
am lonesome all day thinking about it.*[23]

❧

❧ Lullaby

Shall I take the rainbow out of the sky
And the moon from the well in the lane,
And break them in pieces to coax your eye
To slumber a wee while again?
Rock goes the cradle, and rock, and rock.
The mouse has stopped nibbling under the clock
And the crows have gone home to Slane.

The little lambs came from the hills of brown,
With pillows of wool for your fair little head.
And the birds from the bushes flew in with down
To make you snug in your cradle bed.

---

23 Letter to Lizzie about a dream he had

Rock goes the cradle, and rock, and rock.
The mouse has stopped nibbling under the clock
And the birds and the lambs have fled.

There is wind from the bog. It will blow all night,
Upsetting the willows and scattering rain.
The poor little lambs will be crying with fright
For the kind little birds in the hedge of the lane.
Rock goes the cradle, and rock, and rock.
Sleep, little one, sleep, and the wet wind mock,
Til the crows come back from Slane.[24]

---

24 Written for Lizzie's nephew

❦ France 1917

'And now I'm drinking wine in France
The helpless child of circumstance
Tomorrow will be loud with war
How will I be accounted for?'

I am writing this under the most inept circumstances, between my watches, for I am in the firing line and may be busy at any moment in the horrible work of war.[25]

❧

☞ The Dead Kings

All the dead kings came to me
At Rosnaree, where I was dreaming.
A few stars glimmered through the morn,
And down the thorn the dews were streaming.

And every dead king had a story
Of ancient glory, sweetly told.
It was too early for the lark,
But the starry dark had tints of gold.

I listened to the sorrows three
Of that Eire passed into song.
A cock crowed near a hazel croft,
And up aloft dim larks winged strong.

---

25 Letter to Professor Chase

And I, too, told the kings a story
Of later glory, her fourth sorrow:
There was a sound like moving shields
In high green fields and the lowland furrow.

And one said: 'We who yet are kings
Have heard these things lamenting inly'.
Sweet music flowed from many a bill
And on the hill the morn stood queenly.

And one said: 'Over is the singing,
And bell bough ringing, whence we come;
With heavy hearts we'll tread the shadows,
In honey meadows birds are dumb'.

And one said: 'Since the poets perished
And all they cherished in the way,
Their thoughts unsung, like petal showers
Inflame the hours of blue and grey'.

And one said: 'A loud tramp of men
We'll hear again at Rosnaree'.
A bomb burst near me where I lay.
I woke, 'twas day in Picardy.

You ask me what I am doing. I am a unit in the Great War, doing and suffering, admiring great endeavour and condemning great dishonour. I may be dead before this reaches you, but I will have done my part. Death is as interesting to me as life. I have seen so much of it from Suvla to Serbia and now in France. I am always homesick. I hear the roads calling, and the hills, and the rivers wondering where I am. It is terrible to be always homesick.[26]

∽

⤖ Home

A burst of sudden wings at dawn,
Faint voices in a dreamy noon,
Evenings of mist and murmurings,
And nights with rainbows of the moon.

And through these things a wood-way dim,
And waters dim, and slow sheep seen
On uphill paths that wind away
Through summer sounds and harvest green.

---

26 Letter to Katherine Tynan, January 1917

This is a song a robin sang
This morning on a broken tree,
It was about the little fields
That call across the world to me.[27]

⁂

We are under an hour's notice. Entering and leaving the line is most exciting, as we are usually but about thirty yards from the enemy, and you can scarcely understand how bright the nights are made by his rockets. These are in continual ascent and descent from dusk to dawn, making a beautiful crescent from Switzerland to the sea. There are white lights, green, and red, and whiter, bursting into red and changing again, and blue bursting into purple drops and reds fading into green. It is all like the end of a beautiful world. It is only horrible when you remember that every colour is a signal to waiting reinforcements of artillery and God help us if we are caught in the open, for then up go a thousand reds, and hundreds of rifles and machine-guns are emptied against us, and all amongst us shells of every calibre are thrown, shouting destruction and death. We can do nothing but fling ourselves into the first shell-hole and wonder as we wait where we will be hit.[28]

---

27 Inspired by hearing a robin's song at Ypres during a lull in the bombing
28 Letter to Katherine Tynan, May 1917

Ascension Thursday, 1917

Lord, Thou hast left Thy footprints in the rocks
That we may know the way to follow Thee,
But there are wide lands opened out between
Thy Olivet and my Gethsemane.

And oftentimes I make the night afraid,
Crying for lost hands when the dark is deep,
And strive to reach the sheltering of Thy love
Where Thou are herd among Thy folded sheep.

Thou wilt not ever thus, O Lord, allow
My feet to wander when the sun is set,
But through the darkness, let me still behold
The stony bye-ways up to Olivet.

❧ Longing for Home

'The hills of home are in my mind
And there I wander as I will'

To come to things that matter – how are you? And how is your mother? How is trade and Tessie Wall? Remember me to her. I think I have a postcard somewhere, if so I will send it to her. She is a real good sort. I often fancy myself at your door talking to her about the foolish things of our youth.

I hear the Russians are in Germany. God send they may bring this war to a hasty termination and let me home again. I am drifting far away from Slane, far, far. Remember me to everyone I know. Does W. Corbally still come in the morning and Jack McGuirk for his brown cake? I keep always remembering the little things.[29]

❧

❧ The Hills

The hills are crying from the fields to me,
And calling me with music from a choir
Of waters in their woods where I can see
The bloom unfolded on the whins like fire.
And as the evening moon climbs ever higher
And blots away the shadows from the slope,
They cry to me like things devoid of hope.

---

29 Letter to Bobby Anderson in Slane

Pigeons are home. Day droops. The fields are cold.
Now a slow wind comes labouring up the sky
With a small cloud long steeped in sunset gold,
Like Jason with the precious fleece anigh
The harbour of Iolcos. Day's bright eye
Is filmed with the twilight, and the rill
Shines like a scimitar upon the hill.

And moonbeams drooping thro' the coloured wood
Are full of little people wingéd white.
I'll wander through the moon-pale solitude
That calls across the intervening night
With river voices at their utmost height,
Sweet as rain-water in the blackbird's flute
That strikes the world in admiration mute.

I don't think the war can last very long now. Do you ever see Tully? How is Navan? Remember me to the pump on the market square when next you go there, and the clock over Walshe's. Just now I fancy I see Biddy Finnegan sitting on Noonan's window-sill and the thought brings pleasant recollections.[30]

---

30   Letter to Paddy Healy, 1915

You are in Meath now, I suppose. If you go to Tara, go to Rath-na-Rí *and look all round you from the hills of Drumcondrath in the north to the plains of Enfield in the south, where Allen Bog begins, and remember me to every hill and wood and ruin, for my heart is there. If it is a clear day you will see Slane Hill blue and distant. Say I will come back again surely, and maybe you will hear pipes in the grass, or a fairy horn and the hounds of Finn. I have heard them often from Tara.*[31]

It must be quite beautiful on the bog now. How happy you are to be living in peace and quietude where birds still sing and the country wears her confirmation dress. Out here the land is broken up by shells and the woods are like skeletons, and when you come to a little town it is only to find poor homeless people lamenting over what was once a cheery home. As I write this a big battle is raging on my left hand and if it extends to this part of the line I will be pulling triggers like a man gone mad.

Please, dear Lizzie, send me a flower from the bog, plucked specially for me. I may be home again soon. In fact I am only waiting to be called home. God send it soon.[32]

---

31 Letter to Katherine Tynan, June 1917
32 Letter to Lizzie Healy, July 1917

✑ From 'The Place'

And when the war is over I shall take
My lute a-down to it and sing again
Songs of the whispering things amongst the brake,
And those I love shall know them by their strain.
Their airs shall be the blackbird's twilight song,
Their words shall be all flowers with fresh dews hoar.
But it is lonely now in winter long,
And God! to hear the blackbird sing once more.

I daresay you have left Meath and are back again in the brown wilds of Connaught. I would give £100 for two days in Ireland with nothing to do but ramble on from one delight to another. I am entitled to a leave now, but I'm afraid there are many before my name on the list. Special leaves are granted, and I have to finish a book for the autumn. But, more particularly, I want to see again my wonderful mother, and to walk by the Boyne to Crewbawn and up through the brown and grey rocks of Crocknaharna. You have no idea of how I suffer with this longing for the swish of the reeds at Slane and the voices I used to hear coming over the low hills of Currabwee. Say a prayer that I may get this leave, and give as a condition my punctual return and sojourn till the war is over. It is midnight now and

the glow-worms are out. It is quiet in camp, but the far night is loud with our guns bombarding the positions we must soon fight for.[33]

33   Letter to Katherine Tynan (possibly his last letter), 20 July 1917

❧ Death

'And here where that sweet poet sleeps
I hear the songs he left unsung'

'It is believed that a certain immortality awaits those who sing sweetly and die before their prime.'

Obituary on Ledwidge by Professor Lewis Chase

Dear Mrs Ledwidge,

I do not know how to write to you about the death of your dear son, Francis. Quite apart from his wonderful gifts, he was such a lovable boy and I was so fond of him. We had many talks together and he used to read me his poems. He died on the feast of St Ignatius Loyola. The evening before he died he had been to Confession. On the morning of the thirty-first he was present at Mass and received Holy Communion. That evening while out with a working party a shell exploded quite near to them, killing seven and wounding twelve. Francis was killed at once so that he suffered no pain. I like to think that God took him before the world had been able to spoil him with its praise and he has found far greater joy and beauty than ever he would have found on earth. May God comfort you and may His Holy Mother pray for you. I shall say a Mass for Francis as soon as I can.

Charles Henry Devas, S.J.[34]

---

34 Letter to Ledwidge's mother from his army chaplain, Fr Devas S.J.

'He has left behind him verses of great beauty, simple rural lyrics that may be something of an anodyne for this stricken age. If ever an age needed beautiful little songs our age needs them; and I know few songs more peaceful and happy, or better suited to soothe the scars on the mind of those who have looked on certain places, of which the prophecy in the gospels seems no more than an ominous hint when it speaks of the abomination of desolation.'

Lord Dunsany, Introduction to 'Last Songs'

My best is not yet written. I mean to do something really good if I am spared, but out here one may at any moment be hurled beyond life.[35]

'As, still stunned by the news of his death, I look upon his delicate handwriting, there seems to me to have passed from the earth a very rare and

---

35 Ledwidge letter to Professor Chase

promising spirit. Lord Dunsany prophesied better than he knew when he said that all of Francis Ledwidge's future books "lie on the knees of the gods".'

Lewis Chase Obituary

'I was passing through the village and I noticed a little group of people around the post office. I didn't approach them because I was really apprehensive that something was wrong. They were all looking in my direction. I made my way home but I knew Frank was gone, and unfortunately it was I that had to break the news to my mother. It's something indeed I don't like to recall now. It's still too deep for us.'

Joe Ledwidge

A Soldier's Grave

Then in the lull of midnight, gentle arms
Lifted him slowly down the slopes of death,
Lest he should hear again the mad alarms
Of battle, dying moans, and painful breath.

And where the earth was soft for flowers we made
A grave for him that he might better rest.
So, Spring shall come and leave it sweet arrayed,
And there the lark shall turn her dewy nest.

❧ Seamus Heaney

'I think of you in your Tommy's uniform
A haunted Catholic face pallid and brave'

❧ In Memoriam Francis Ledwidge

killed in France 31 July 1917

The bronze soldier hitches a bronze cape
That crumples stiffly in imagined wind
No matter how the real winds buff and sweep
His sudden hunkering run, forever craned

Over Flanders. Helmet and haversack,
The gun's firm slope from butt to bayonet,
The loyal, fallen names on the embossed plaque –
It all meant little to the worried pet

I was in nineteen forty-six or seven,
Gripping my Aunt Mary by the hand
Along the Portstewart prom, then round the crescent
To thread the Castle Walk out to the strand.

The pilot from Coleraine sailed to the coal-boat.
Courting couples rose out of the scooped dunes
A farmer stripped to his studs and shiny waistcoat
Rolled the trousers down on his timid shins.

Francis Ledwidge, you courted at the seaside
Beyond Drogheda one Sunday afternoon.
Literary, sweet-talking, countrified,
You pedalled out the leafy road from Slane

Where you belonged, among the dolorous
And lovely: the May altar of wild flowers,
Easter water sprinkled in outhouses,
Mass-rocks and hill-top raths and raftered byres.

I think of you in your Tommy's uniform,
A haunted Catholic face, pallid and brave,
Ghosting the trenches with a bloom of hawthorn
Or silence cored from a Boyne passage-grave.

It's summer, nineteen-fifteen. I see the girl
My aunt was then, herding on the long acre.
Behind a low bush in the Dardanelles
You suck stones to make your dry mouth water.

It's nineteen-seventeen. She still herds cows
But a big strafe puts the candles out in Ypres:
'My soul is by the Boyne, cutting new meadows …
My country wears her confirmation dress.'

'To be called a British soldier while my country
Has no place among nations …' You were rent
By shrapnel six weeks later. 'I am sorry
That party politics should divide our tents.'

In you, our dead enigma, all the strains
Criss-cross in useless equilibrium

And as the wind tunes through this vigilant bronze
I hear again the sure confusing drum

You followed from Boyne water to the Balkans
But miss the twilit note your flute should sound.
You were not keyed or pitched like these true-blue ones
Though all of you consort now underground.[36]

✒ Francis Ledwidge: An Assessment*

In my poem 'In Memoriam – Francis Ledwidge', I refer to
the poet as 'our dead enigma'. I am thinking of Ledwidge
being associated in the popular mind with one poem in
particular, the 'Lament for Thomas McDonagh' – which is
very much an Irish nationalist, separatist, Gaelic sentiment
– and at the same time his being an enlisted member of
the British Army and fighting alongside the Redmondite
recruits to that army. He was highly conscious of his own
dilemma:

*To be called a British soldier while my country
Has no place among nations …*

But I think he is most interesting because of a kind of
moral fortitude that he bore. He is an example of the 'poet
as witness' – a phrase we tend to associate with poets in
Soviet Russia or the Eastern bloc – but he actually joined
the army because of a certain visionary, noble, moral side
to his nature. In his letter to Professor Chase he is aware
of all the complications and of the figure he is cutting in
the imaginations and minds of his friends at home who
belonged to the Irish Volunteers:

* This is an edited transcript of a radio interview conducted in 1987 between Seamus
Heaney and John Quinn

Some of the people who know me least imagine that I joined the Army because I knew men were struggling for higher ideals and great emprises, and I could not sit idle to watch them make for me a more beautiful world. They are mistaken. I joined the British Army because she stood between Ireland and an enemy common to our civilisation and I would not have her say that she defended us while we did nothing at home but pass resolutions …

There is a kind of majesty in those words, an acceptance of both responsibility and of division. He is fighting for the honour of Ireland, but in a complicated way. In order to save that honour he has to join the British Army. I don't think that is the mark of a man who was cajoled by rhetoric. There is another notion that he was cajoled by Lord Dunsany into joining the army. I don't think that notion stands up. The evidence of his statement suggests that he was a man who accepted responsibility for his actions and that he knew the complicated nature of what he was doing.

He was a member of Navan Rural District Council. There was a split in the council over the Irish Volunteers versus the National Volunteers. Ledwidge was associated with the Irish Volunteers, the separatist wing, defending them against a majority of the council in the course of a number of meetings. Then suddenly he joins the British

Army. That is not the act of a simple-minded yea-sayer, floated in the wake of majority decisions. It is a very personal act of witness.

I find Ledwidge touching as a poet. Apart from a few poems like the 'Lament for Thomas McDonagh' and 'The Wife of Llew' – which is more or less a direct translation from the Welsh 'Mabinogion' – his poetry is pleasing but of its time. There is an unsophisticated, literary, sentimental, rural note in the poems, which is continuous with the Poet's Corner in a local newspaper. I think Ledwidge was patronised in both senses by Lord Dunsany, but the fact of the matter is that through the poetry path Ledwidge arrived at a kind of maturity, a kind of grip on the nature of our ambiguous experience in modern Ireland as a country wishing for separate status but also as a country which – if it takes that wish too far – becomes isolationist and maintains a culpable ignorance in the modern world. Ledwidge was against that culpable ignorance. He was for us taking our place among the nations of the world.

It is often remarked that despite his direct engagement with the horrors of war, those horrors never seemed to impinge on Ledwidge's poetry. This was a common phenomenon and it was only among artists of the highest order that the experience of war forged a particular style. The most difficult thing in the world is to find a form for what is going on. Usually when people are writing they do so in a mode that is supplied by previous writing and this would be especially so in the case of an unsophisticated, obedient writer like Ledwidge. It requires considerable imagination and re-thinking to find a language for what is real and new. With the exception of Wilfred Owen and Siegfried Sassoon, most of the poetry written in the trenches of World War I was the poetry of what has been called 'pastoral recourse' i.e. you compensate for the horrific conditions by remembering the pastoral. The psyche flees from the awful into the desirable, so most of the poetry of that time was of memories of pre-war pastoral Eden-like conditions. Ledwidge was not at all alone in being an example of that.

He is a tender, beautiful figure, walking in a mist of melancholy. He has been cherished in Ireland for a number of reasons. Firstly, he was completely unthreatening to a culture that was dominated by Catholic schools and Gaelic sentiment. You could give a volume of Ledwidge to your aunt, a reverend mother or a convent girl without raising a blush! He had that Catholic safety about him which ensured his official admittance in the Twenties, Thirties and Forties. Secondly, he had a patriotic aura, having written about Thomas McDonagh and having that Gaelic note running through his work.

His status and popularity in our pantheon have to do with extra-poetic reasons. It is based on poetry, of course, but it is boosted by our affection for what we see as something innocent, vulnerable and brave in him. And there is something really wonderful in the stamina and determination of a young country lad in his achievement of a quality of civility in himself, at a time when self-improvement was in the air.

There was a devastating difference between conditions in the trenches and conditions at home, a few hours away. In fact, officers could slip home for a weekend away from the trenches. But for the vast majority to recognise a new reality and admit it into the currency of language and into consciousness was too big an act. We know of thousands and thousands who came home and couldn't speak of their experience – 'It was just the war.' That is one of the reasons you could say – and without blame – that Ledwidge is a minor writer. I don't think he would have managed to register the change, if he had lived.

It is important to celebrate Ledwidge because he is an example of that specifically twentieth-century, heroic kind of writer – the writer as witness. His writings and actions imply solidarity with wretched and complicated conditions. He did achieve poetic form, particularly in his definitive elegy for McDonagh. He was part of a moment in our literary history when native themes and native landscape were becoming current. You would have to think of him alongside writers like Padraic Colum and

AE. He is a contributor to our common memory and is therefore to be honoured.

❧ Sources

Francis Ledwidge: Complete Poems
Edited by Alice Curtayne, Martin Brian & O'Keefe,
London 1974

Francis Ledwidge: A Life of the Poet
Alice Curtayne, Martin Brian & O'Keefe, London 1972

Francis Ledwidge: Obituary
Professor Lewis Chase, University of Rochester, N.Y.
The Cornhill Magazine, London, June 1920

Interview with Seamus Heaney
by John Quinn, Dublin 1987

The Helpless Child of Circumstance
Radio Documentary produced by John Quinn
RTÉ Radio, December 1987

Opened Ground: Selected Poems 1966-1996
Seamus Heaney, Faber & Faber, London 1998